The Other Side of Suicide

by
Karen Peebles

OZARK
MOUNTAIN
PUBLISHING

Library of Congress Cataloging-in-Publication Data
Karen Peebles - 1966 -
"The Other Side of Suicide" by Karen Peebles
Information from the other realm of what happens when you commit suicide. Information for families of persons who have ended their lives early. Healing and learning that takes place after you die.

1. Suicide 2. Life after Death 3. Reincarnation
I. Karen Peebles, 1966 - II. Title

Library of Congress Catalog Control Number:
ISBN: 978-1-886940-60-4

Cover Design: enki3d.com
Book Design: Julia Degan
Book Set in: Times New Roman, Parchment

Published By

OZARK MOUNTAIN PUBLISHING

PO Box 754, Huntsville, AR 72740
800-935-0045 or 479-738-2348 fax: 479-738-2448

WWW.OZARKMT.COM
Printed in the United States of America

Table of Contents

Introduction by George

Readers, I crossed over and into the spirit world 25 years ago, having ended my life prematurely by what you call on Earth suicide. You would call me a suicide victim.

I have a lot to say, having been here now for this long and having looked all of that time for someone there on Earth to communicate with. Someone to bring back the knowledge that I now have access to and share that knowledge with persons, like the person I was while alive, who have lost hope and feel so heavily burdened by life that only death itself seems like a solution.

I also have much that I want to share with families of persons who have ended their lives early.

While I reside now, here in the spirit realm, I have a greater understanding of the mechanics of life on Earth. Why we choose to come down to Earth to begin with, how we allow ourselves to get caught up in the world of illusion, and how we can easily lose touch with the true essence of who we really are while living on the Earth; which is what happens all too often and escalates to the point of a desire to end life before its perfect time.

Allow me, if you will readers, to take you back to the exact moment of my crossing over from life as you know it, to this realm of the spirit. Give me the chance to open your minds to new thoughts and ideas that you have never dared to think before.

It is my intention to reveal the mystery of suicide, to expel the untruths about it that are popular conceptions on Earth. To explore a new avenue, one that has not been looked at before quite in this way.

Prologue by Karen Peebles

Twenty-five years ago I received a terrible phone call that was most unlooked for, a call to let me know that my Uncle George had committed suicide. The shock of that type of call is immeasurable. You truly cannot put your finger down and pinpoint the dominant emotion of that moment.

I can remember a mixture of anger and grief, although I don't understand where the anger actually came from, it was definitely one of the greater emotions. There was a great deal of confusion amidst the grieving as well.

I have struggled for quite a lot of years since that phone call – struggled within my own mind. Wondering, what makes a person lose hope so completely. Wondering, where does the soul of a suicide victim go to after life. Wondering, what their families must go through. Yes, wondering, for so many years…

It was late in my life that I learned that there were many gifts of the psyche unexplored within me, waiting to be unfolded.

It was in the Fall of 2005 when I discovered I could contact my father who had died 10 years prior to that time. Finding that piece of information – learning that I could contact the dead – I grasped onto it tightly and spent countless hours with him, talking, laughing again, learning from him.

It was during one of our long talks that my father told me that I was able to visit with my Uncle George if I desired to.

– if I desired to –

"Where is George?" I asked my dad.

"George is nearby," he said to me, and although I wasn't certain what he meant by that, I was soon to find out the answers to more questions than I could conjure up, which is quite a lot, I can tell you.

This book is a compilation of many, many hours worth of conversations that I have had with my Uncle George, who tells me to call him George now. This book was his idea, and while I had initially told him that I was not the person he had spent 25 years looking for to bring this knowledge through, he assured me at that time that "Some things are true whether or not you believe in them."

This then, is the collection of information from the spirit known as George, who ended his life early while on the Earth and seeks to impart a greater knowledge to others who are contemplating the same fate.

Not Yet –
The Abortion of Suicide

Chapter 1 in the
Life After Suicide Trilogy

I want to begin this book by plainly stating a universal truth – you exist. There is nothing, and I want to repeat, nothing, that can stop you from existing. You can choose to end your life early, but you will continue to exist.

Please be aware that "suicide" is a term that is used by society as a whole to define the early ending of a person's life before their natural time.

The term suicide is such a cold and impersonal word, it can even be used to define a person who had ended their life early, as in "a suicide". It is not, however, a term used here in the realm where I exist. We have no such term for the soul of a human being who leaves his body before it is time to. We have only unconditional love for such a soul.

It is my great desire to bring knowledge to the Earth that I have been given to understand since my crossing over into the spirit world – knowledge that I feel would be helpful to people and to families who are suffering from the stigma of suicide. For you see, it is the "stigma" of ending one's life early that causes much of the grief that families must endure long after the death of their loved one. It is the "stigma" that attaches itself to a person who has ended their life early, that creates in and around that person the identity of a suicide victim.

Because of the stigma attached to suicide, the *family* of a person who has ended their life out of time does not suffer a typical loss, as, say, the family of a person who dies from a heart attack, or an accident. They will suffer a double loss, one far greater than a regular death because this death must forever be kept silent in their hearts or spoken of in hushed tones.

When a man or woman, a boy or a girl commits suicide, people tend to familiarize them with the event. They tend to see suicide in all aspects of the person. Then they fail to remain the brilliant musician, or the budding artist, or the aspiring young person that they were, but now they have attached to them this stigma of suicide that defines them anew.

If you notice that I have used that word "stigma" quite a few times now, it is by no accident, it is to show you that the stigma is actual, it is real, and that it is a thing that does much damage and creates much needless grief for the family.

This is a grave mistake for family and friends to make, to attach that stigma on to the person's identity.

Ending one's life prematurely does not erase that person's life. It does not discredit them from accomplishments they have achieved, by any means.

Before I had my first visit with George in our place of meeting that I call the workshop, I had many questions for my father about where George was now residing and what conditions he was living under. Sadly, I had been brought up to think that the souls of humans who took their own lives could never be in the light of God. I now know that this is a misguided belief and a wrong teaching, especially one to impart toward children.

My father gave me a brief description of what he has seen happen to the souls of humans just crossing over who had ended their life early. This is what he told me:

"Upon crossing over, souls of humans who have ended their lives early are immediately surrounded by high spirits who begin work on the soul to rebuild their self-esteem and character. They are given the opportunity to look at their lives on Earth in sequence and learn from their past actions.

It is not at all what you think for them. Only on Earth is there the taboo in regards to what you call suicide. Here, it is just the opposite. It is those souls who need the most nurturing and extreme love, which is what they receive. They are not judged by their final actions. They are given understanding and the greatest compassion."

During my first visit with George, I was absolutely amazed that he was very different than I remembered him in life. First, he was much younger in the spirit world. He looked to be in his thirties. His mannerisms were much the same, but his character was of a gentler nature. There were distinct things about him that I could pick out that he had been working on within himself. He was a kinder, gentler version of the same man that I remember.

I had so many questions I wanted to ask him, but I was afraid to ask them for fear of asking in the wrong way. I didn't know how to approach the subject.

On one visit, George took me aside and said to me, "Listen Karen, it's no secret that I ended my life. A secret is something that only a few people know about and they keep it hushed. But everyone knows that I ended my life. It's not a secret when everyone knows."

Then he took my hands and looked in my eyes. "Don't be afraid to ask me what you want to ask."

This made me feel tremendously comfortable and relaxed enough to ask many questions about his life in the spirit world.

One of the greatest insights I have learned in the workshop from various visitors is that spirits are not idle, they have much to do. Several of the spirits I have spoken to in that realm have told me about the work that they are involved in. Some of them have described how they work with people down here on Earth almost as angels to assist them in their lives and work. Others tell me that they work with spirits who are just crossing over into the spirit realm, helping them to make the adjustments from one plane to the next. My grandmother tells me that she works with children, both on Earth and in the spirit world.

On one of the visits to the workshop, I asked George what he is doing now with his life. I thought that perhaps he had a certain type of work as did the other spirits I had asked.

"I have not yet moved on from where I was first placed after I came here.
Don't look like that! It is not a solemn thing. There is no taboo here. That is only on the planet where you live. Here where I am, it is a beautiful place, a ward you might call it. I am becoming the man I always knew I could be. The man I could have been.

I am growing in ways I did not know I was able to, and sharing that with those who now need that.

I have been, 25 years, searching for the person with whom I could communicate, who would take this knowledge back to the Earth to help others who are contemplating the same that I was.

When I find that person that I am able to connect with, I will move on from this ward and begin my work.

Karen, are you that person?"

I told George that I was not that person he had been waiting for all those years, but I did tell him that I would assist him in the writing of a book if he would give me a few months to straighten out some things in my life first. I am well aware of the amount of time writing a book can take out of your life.

He agreed to co-author a book with me, but he didn't wait several months to begin imparting the information. He began that very night. He told me to get notebooks ready and he started talking until it was well past 2 in the morning. I finally had to tell him to stop talking for Pete's sake. I had to get up early the next morning with my kids.

"When you want to meet with me Karen, go into your Bird Room and take a left at Pompeii. You will see an archway that you've never noticed before. We will meet there at your convenience to work on the book." [1]

Unfortunately, after 25 years, George was in a hurry to get things moving. For the first several nights after discussing the idea of the book, he would start talking to me as soon as I closed my eyes at night to go to sleep. He rarely stopped talking until long after 2.

He would tell me to go get my notebooks, to make sure the pens were writing properly. He seemed so pent up with

---

1. The Bird Room is a place in my mind where I meditate. Pompeii is my pet cockatoo that lives in the Bird Room.

ideas and knowledge, I would write his words down as quickly as I could, but he never seemed to get tired.

I could feel his passion for what he was doing. I understood his need to take what he now knew and bring that wisdom back to Earth for others to benefit from.

Every now and then I would remind him that I was not the person he had been waiting for. That I was only there to assist him in the writing of the book.

And he would smile at me with a knowing smile and say very little.

It hurt me a little inside, that he truly felt I was the one, when I knew that I was not.

I began making lists of the questions that I would ask George when we met at the little room he told me about (left at Pompeii in the Bird Room).

It was three nights after our decision to begin the book, and I was getting myself tucked in for the night and ready to journey down to the Bird Room to meet with George. Upon greeting my beautiful friend Pompeii at step 4, I immediately took the left and continued on for the remainder of the 12 steps that it takes to get out of the Bird Room. I walked under the misty archway, and there-in I found myself entering a small room with a balcony on the far end.

George was there, out on the balcony, waving for me to come out with him, smiling at me and excited that I had decided to meet with him.

As I walked out of the room, through plate glass doors that led out to the balcony, I saw beyond the balcony and downward a beautiful white sand beach with seagulls flying overhead of the breakers. I could smell the ocean air and feel the breeze coming off of the surf.

"I'm very happy that you decided to come and meet with me tonight."

"This is a beautiful place that you picked for the writing of the book," I told him.

We both sat down at a small table that was set up on the balcony, and George told me to get my notebooks ready to write down what he had to say.

"Karen, that you would bring back this knowledge, to transcend the veil with this knowledge, that is an incredible thing. Let me give you a shocker. You *are* the person I have waited for, to assist me in bringing this wisdom to the Earth.

You doubt that you are a medium. What do you think you are doing right now?"

"Having committed suicide does not define who I am. Neither am I the sum total of my past actions.

When I ended my life, and crossed over into the spirit world, there was an almost instant recognition that I had had other options before me that I chose to ignore.

There was desperation from recognizing that fact. There was tremendous regret, confusion, and a sense of deep loss of myself.

Then, the way that I was surrounded by such healing beings of spirit, it is indescribable for me to tell you. I was enveloped in their care, rebuilt from the inside out, with no portion left unaided.

I was given the unique opportunity to see again my life, aspects of my life, choices I had made, decisions. I was not judged, but I was given this to learn from. To grow by.

The ward that I was placed in is a beautiful place. I am still here by my own choosing. I could have left long ago when they were through with what they did for me, but then, I see these kids coming in, like I first did, and I thought that if I can do for them what was done for me, then I want to have a part in that.

Then I thought to myself, that if I could do that for them while they are still on the Earth, then that would be the thing to do. If I could bring that to them before they make their decision.

I made up my mind that I would try to bring them what is offered here at the ward – total acceptance, understanding. Not question them, but give to them. That is my work here. Now I have begun to move on."

"Do you mean that you are no longer in the ward?"

"Oh yes, I am still here, but it's different now. Imagine this. Imagine waking up in a hospital after a terrible accident and finding out that a great surgeon has just saved your life by the skill of his hands. That he put you back together on the inside and on the out. That he utterly saved you. You marvel at this knowing. While you are healing, there at the hospital, you develop the desire to heal others as this doctor healed you.

Your healing is slow, because your wounds were so deep. And while you heal, you think, always think of helping others in the same way. You dream of it always, until it becomes a passion of yours.

So you watch the surgeon over all the long years that you are there at the hospital. What deep wounds you must have suffered to have been there all these years and not have left yet. You watch the surgeon and you learn, until you feel that you are ready. That you can now do what he does.

What do you think now? If I became the surgeon, would I still be at the ward? I would be, in a sense, but I would have also moved on.

So yes, Karen, I am here at the ward, but I am no new-comer to this place. I have watched these spirits in amazement as they work what can only be called a miraculous transformation within the tenants of this ward. Just notice the transformation in me! See what they have done!

While I remain here, I will move on now, for the time is right to do that.

"That is quite enlightening. I'm getting a better picture now of where you reside. Thank you for that picture. Can you share with me some of that knowledge that you spoke of which you said would be helpful to persons here on Earth who are contemplating ending their lives early?"

"Yes. First, I want to tell you that I am linked to them. To every individual that is in that state of mind. I am bound to them emotionally and mentally. That may be hard for you to understand. Because of my intentions, and because of theirs, we are bound.

Now I know that many of the things I have to say are not going to be easily accepted by you, and may seem as though I am advocating the early ending of life. That will only seem so because you do not have the understanding that we have here. There on Earth, suicide is the unforgivable sin. Here, in the spirit realm, it is an act of desperation. It is truly the forgivable act. By it's very nature, it warrants forgiveness and love.

On Earth, you have a vested interest in scaring the unfortunate person who is already under torment of the spirit and mind. Scaring them into thinking that if they do this – if they end their life – they are doomed. Your interest is in keeping them there on the Earth for selfish purposes. To keep them near you. To keep them living because death is too scary for you to think about.

These are all wrong thoughts. They do nothing to help the person who is going through this trial. They do nothing to help you either. They will serve only to confuse.

A person who is thinking about ending their life needs from you, foremost, the freedom to decide for themselves if that is what they are going to do. Heaping guilt atop of all that they are carrying around just might be the weight that puts them over their limit. Release them from that guilt though, and you will find a lighter mind. One that is more able to make a good decision.

Let me ask the reader this. Are you someone who knows for certain that a loved one is contemplating suicide? Are you terrified to talk to them about it? Why are you? Ask them about it. Tell them that you know. Talking about death can be as natural as talking about life. You have to go to a new place in your mind. Find newer ways to think about life and death. Your old ways are not serving your society.

Do you want to prevent suicide? You must first learn to talk about it amongst yourselves. You will never learn to prevent it if you cannot even speak about it.

If you have a loved one that is struggling with thoughts of suicide, you can do one very important thing for them. You can stop thinking about yourself. Stop fearing what will happen to you if they end their life. What will people say? How will you live with the grief? Stop worrying about yourself. The death of another human being has absolutely nothing to do with you. It has only to do with them.

Now the point is to get you to switch that energy away from yourself and toward the other person. It is their life that they are thinking about ending. It is their life and choice. Not yours.

Do you really want to help them? Then tell them so! Tell them that it is their life and choice. Nothing could be truer than that. Give them the dignity of allowing them to make their own choice.

Now, if you are a person who is thinking about ending your life, let me add my insights to yours.

If you think there is nothing on the other side of death but blackness and void – you are mistaken. There is life, of a newer kind.

If you think that suicide will end your problems there on the Earth – you are correct. But your correct-ness is not complete. Your knowledge about the problems that pose themselves there on Earth is not accurate. You have drawn those problems to yourself as challenges for personal growth. If you no longer want those challenges, then turn from them. Choose that growth later.

If you believe that ending your life early will doom you to exist in hell – you are wrong. Yet know that hell has many meanings.

If you think your problems on the Earth are too great for you to bear – you are looking at life through narrow eyes.

If you are trying to teach someone else a lesson by threatening suicide – know that they will not learn what you wish them to.

If you are looking for the silence of the grave in death – you will not find it. Your spirit does not reside within the grave.

If you feel certain that you cannot live with yourself after committing acts of crime or atrocity, let me assure you that you are not who you were yesterday. You are the person you are becoming.

If you are tired of living – take a nap.

Ending your life early because of problems that seem too much to deal with – which is by and far the major reason for wanting to leave this life – is like throwing out the baby with the bath water. It can be difficult in life to see problems that surround you as temporary. They can feel and seem as though they are your life itself. Do not confuse your problems with your process of life, which is on-going, which is permanent, which is everlasting.

Life continues on, it is eternal. Try to look above the horizons of your life and see the troubles you now face as a fog that is hovering closely above your life, blurring your vision. But wait! Sooner or later a strong breeze, which is the process of life, it's very essence, will move those troubles out and away from your horizon and clear your path of vision again.

Do you see that the turmoil, the sadness, the worry, the heart-ache, poverty, sickness, all of the things in life that you fear and loathe, they can not last? For life is not stagnant. Nothing in life can stay the same. It must, by definition of itself, change in order to fulfill the procession of its nature. As it is with your life. You are no exception to that rule.

If you can manage to rise above those horizons of your own sight, look down at your life, at yourself, in a new way, you will overcome the impermanence as what you perceive are problems with no way out.

Do you think that it is easier said than done? That those are easy words coming from a man who no longer lives within the struggles and confines of the real world?

Let me tell you something. *This* is the real world. Here, where I am. The spirit world.

You are living in the world of illusion. You have allowed the insignificances of your world – however huge they seem to you – to rule your conscious. You have taken part in the great game of life, which is something we have all agreed to upon beginning our lives, yet you have created confusion between the game itself and who you really are. You are not the game. You are pure spirit, playing out the game.

How do I know that? I know it because I did the same thing. In life, I allowed trivial matters to cloud up my judgment and take over my thinking; those trivial matters, seemed at the time that they were my life itself.

I want to explain to you what will happen the exact moment of your crossing over, should you decide to end your life. The instant that you leave your world and cross over into mine, you will immediately recognize the error of your judgment. Your regret will be complete.

You will remember the reason that you originally decided to be born on the Earth, which has been lost to you since your birth. You will remember this reason, and will be able to see how small were your obstacles in life in comparison to the goals you had once set for yourself before beginning your life.

There will be a tearing apart of your emotions while you try to get back into your body, but understand that there is no way to cross back over, no matter how desperate your attempts to do so.

You will feel the emotions of your loved ones at that time as they find out that you are no longer among the living on planet Earth.

There will be another tearing apart within you as you try to make them understand that you are not dead. Or doomed.

But then, within the blink of an eye, there will be spirits attending to you.

I cannot express to you enough that it is the confusing of the problems in life with life itself that begins to form the error in judgment that leads to suicide.
If you could place a divider between the two of them, in your mind, and build upon that divider, your mind would grow strong again. Your life could move on to a place of stability.

I am so certain that this confusion is the formation of suicide within the mind that I want to diagram for you now a new method of thought. A way to place the divider and continue on with your life in a way that you did not think possible.

I began this book by saying that you exist. I want you to stop what you're doing now and sit quietly and just take a look at yourself, while you exist. Do nothing but breathe and look at yourself. Do that now.

Look at your hands, turn them over and look at their back sides. Look down at your feet and legs. Your whole body. Just breathe, and look. Be conscious of your breath.

You are existing. Right now. You could continue to sit there for hours breathing and existing, even days; acknowledging yourself, breathing, and existing.

Now I want to tell you something. You could do *nothing else* in life, but sit there and breathe, and you would still exist. You could decide not to show up for work again. Not to take part in life at all. You could stop eating, drinking, talking.

Nothing can keep you from existing.

The world can lock you away behind bars, starve you, beat you, throw innumerable challenges at you. Yet nothing can keep you from existing. It is your right. Your nature. To exist.

You might say, "If I sat there until I starved to death, I would stop living."

You would be wrong. You are alive, even at the moment of death, and after.

And so, this is where you draw the dividing line, between your existence and the problems in your life that make you think that life is not worth living. You are not your problems. Neither are you your past. You are the essence of life, and that only.

You have come to think of life's problems as an integration of yourself. You have learned to believe that you are helpless in freeing yourself from them because you believe the problems to be who you are.

Now is the time, to look at all of the aspects in your life, no matter how much they hurt to look at. Those aspects that have brought you to where you are now – to standing this close to wanting to end your life.

Take a good look at them.

Yes, I know it's painful.

Look at them.

Life is too painful to go on living?

Life seems too long to make it to the end?

Life is too hard to go on anymore?

I understand those thoughts and feelings. I can remember thinking them. Feeling them. Don't forget, I've been where you are now. I even took a step farther than you have yet to take.

It is my understanding of the senseless loss in suicide that brought me back, through Karen. My desire to abort the needless ending of even one life, if possible.

Do you know what I see at the ward, being played out a thousand times over every day?

I see the spirits of people crossing over and into our world. The spirits of people who have taken their own lives, coming in to the ward, day in and day out. It never ends. Kids mostly. Kids! They haven't even begun their lives, and yet they think their lives are over! Many of them have not even left home yet and seen the magic of life unfold to them. They have confused the problems of their lives with life itself.

There is nothing in your world to compare to what we see in the ward. We must give love unconditionally, or these new souls would never make it through the beginning stages of their healing. We must begin our work as quickly as possible to introduce to them the forgiveness that they will need in order to be able to forgive themselves.

As I said earlier, there is a tremendous sense of regret on the part of the soul. This regret can tear apart the mind and emotions of the soul, which we must immediately undo and repair.

The crossing over from your world to ours, when the spirit has ended their life, is overwhelming for the spirit, as they are experiencing all of these emotions and thoughts that I have described for you. It is only through a deep understanding on the part of the spirits who work in the ward that progress can take place.

In the glimpses of what happens after the ending of a person's life, you can get an idea of how you would be treated if you decided to go ahead with the ending of your life. You can get an idea of what you would be going through, although my words cannot do it proper justice.

I can guarantee you, that the instant after your death, you would try to be again among the living, futilely, inexpressibly futilely.

Your attempts to soothe the spirits of your loved ones still on Earth will be just as barren. They will have to find healing of their own kind.

You will have all that you can do in the ward to heal yourself of the sickness that you brought with you from your world to ours. It can take years, what you would call years, on Earth.

Am I trying to scare you out of ending your life? Certainly not. I want to make one thing clear to you – the choice is yours, what you will do with your life. That choice does not belong to your parent, your child, your spouse or friend. Not your clergyman or priest. It is yours alone.

It is not my intention to influence you by showing you what you will undergo, should you decide to end your life early.

Yet it is my intention to influence you by telling you what you can yet become should you decide to see what life has in store for you.

It is my intention to create a passion within you for the mystery of your own life.

I am bound to you because of your thoughts and emotions, because of mine. From the spirit world, I look down at life on the Earth and I can see and feel each soul that is thinking and feeling as you are. As I watch them making their decisions, I want to cry out to them "Can't you see beyond the horizons of your own problems?! Can't you see?! Look what lies just around the corner!"

But just as I could not see, I cannot make you see, either.

Yet, there must be a way."

As I met with George over the next couple of weeks, I asked him several times if he could describe the ward to me in further detail. I wanted to understand what it was really like to be there. To work there. To be a new-comer to the ward.

"Take me to the Ward!" I would say to him.

But George told me that I would not survive the vast differences between the highs and lows of energy that exist in the ward. That the diversity of energy would harm me.

"I need to see the ward with my own eyes to be able to write about it," I said to him. "I want to feel what it's like to be there!"

While George said that he could not take me there, he did say there might be another way that I could see it.

Twice, I was given a vision of what it would be like to cross over from this life and into the spirit realm. It was quite overwhelming for me, as I experienced floods of emotion – confusion, desperation, realization that I could not get back into my body. I could feel the emotions of all of my loved ones left on Earth, even though I was not with them at that time. I could feel their grief and sorrow. I could hear their thoughts. Around me, I could see other souls arriving who were confused, as I was. And I saw spirits of multitudes reaching out to comfort them.

As the vision and experience continued on, I had complete knowledge that I was not dead. I understood that what I was feeling and seeing was not actually happening to me, but I was experiencing what would occur should I cross over from suicide. And even then, I was given further understanding that the experience was softened for me, that I was not being allowed to travel through the full gamut of emotion, as that journey would be too much for me to bear in human spirit.

Upon emerging from those two visions, I was no longer able to look on life as I had before. Nothing in life was the same to me after. I had been given the opportunity to see beyond the veil of death to the other side. The chance to feel what it was to be dead. And I have to tell you, death is not being dead. It is just the dawning of a new life.

The confusion and desperation I had felt upon the crossing over was brief. I will say that such a great realization was placed in my mind that looking back at life on Earth was like looking through a magician's trick, finally seeing how the tiger disappeared and laughing at the trick. Being the only one in the room, perhaps, to see through the trick, and looking around at the others still mesmerized by the tiger's disappearance. Wondering how I could have also been mesmerized for so long.

I knew then that life was an illusion. As I had suspected during my life, but could not prove. All of life, with the exception of the love that we offer to others along our way, is illusion placed around us as challenge for personal growth. That the problems we create during our lifetimes are some of the greatest of illusions and some of the hardest to see through. That material objects that we idolize in life are indeed dust in the wind.

I understood, that life is eternal and that what we call life here on Earth is a counterfeit kind of life that we so dearly believe in and try to hold on to for as long as we can. Now, to me, life here on Earth seems like a paper toy, in comparison to the life that awaits us when we leave here.

After those two visions, I went to visit George in that wonderful beachside balcony that we share in the evenings. I told him how grateful I was for the visions and for the opportunity to finally get to know him after all the years of only "knowing" him.

In life, when George would visit our family, I would become invisible until he left, by my own design. I had always felt sad that I never got to know him in life.

Now, I was learning about him in ways that were not available to the two of us while he was alive. I was quite grateful for that.

On the balcony, George would hug me when I would arrive for our visits, which was something I have no memory of him ever doing in life. He would kiss me on the top of my head and thank me for meeting with him to bring this book through.

Even after all I was allowed to see, I continued to ask George to expand on his description of the ward, which simply fascinated me without end.

"Let me take you on a dry run now of what you might experience on crossing over into our realm, should you decide to end your life early.

You have just crossed over and into the spirit world. You have been knocked off of your feet with the knowledge that what you have done is final. There is no going back to continue with unfinished business. You are reeling with remorse.

While dozens of healing spirits reach toward you to comfort you, you are not yet ready to accept the healing. You have much to think first, to feel first, and to realize first.

Yet you will take the healing, and the spirits will wait for you to be receptive of their love.

The ward has rooms of deep and lesser greens, it is like an emerald city to us, vast and beautiful.

When you arrive, you are placed in a brilliant green room that illuminates your emotions and thought.

We have greater knowledge of color and light healing here.

There are many children working throughout the ward whose energies and laughter serve to hasten the healing process.

These spirit children are able to work with suicide victims in a unique way that adult spirits are not able to.

Tenants of the ward are responsive to these children and are able to communicate with them in ways that are self-healing.

Of course, there are adult healers also. Spirits who have dedicated a certain amount of their time and work to the aid of the tenants. They are spirits with a great generosity toward others.

With escorts, newly arriving souls are free to walk throughout the city, and it is encouraged to do so. Upon seeing the incredible number of spirits crossing over daily, souls will gain insight in the incredible waste of life occurring. Seeing first hand the unbelievable numbers arriving is overwhelming to new tenants, which adds to their remorse.

Very quickly, souls are responsive to the healing available to them. It takes only a few walks around our emerald city before newly arriving souls wish to participate in helping other souls that are crossing over.

So much knowledge has been given to them, and so much understanding taken on, that it is natural to wish to give that to the souls who are still confused by the transition.

This is a place of great healing. Your planet has nothing like it in place. Your people do not have the knowledge to build such a facility. Your pre-occupation with financial gain and liability will not allow this degree of nurturing."

"So, are you trying to say that the pre-mature ending of one's life is really all right because their souls will be taken care of when they cross over?"

"I'm trying to tell you that the ending of life pre-maturely is not necessary in order to escape the problems that you face in life. I'm trying to show you how easy it is to get mixed up in your thinking that the problems are life itself, when actually, the problems have nothing to do with who you are, intrinsically. You are spirits of pure being that cannot be extinguished no matter what you attempt to do with or to your physical bodies.

Problems arise throughout your life because you have drawn them to yourself. Your greater conscience seeks out newer challenges. Newer forms of growth. You incarnated because you wanted to do something on Earth, but you have long ago forgotten what that was that you're trying to do.

The problems in life are your soul's attempt to remind you that you are seeking to grow, always to grow.

How can you grow with no challenge before you? How can you learn if life does not hand you a curve ball every now and then?

It's easy to cut out of life early, leaving the problems behind you. Nothing could be easier than to walk away from what does not please you in life.

No. I'm not saying that it's all right to end your life or that it's all wrong to end your life. I'm saying that there are other options that you may not have thought about.

Choose to exist – which by the way you cannot help but do. Choose to exist for just another moment of time. Separate yourself from your problems if you are not interested in that growth right now. And just exist.

Tomorrow you can choose to exist for another day.

If you have been giving any serious thought to ending your life, you will understand that your sense of time does not coincide with the world's any longer because you have already given thought to dying. Time does not tick for you as it does with the rest of the world. You have already been given a taste of what time is like here in our realm.

Find a place. Sit and breathe, and just be. Let the hours roll by, what do you care? You have already considered that the world will still turn without you. Let the hours roll by. Breathe and sit. Sit and breathe. Look at your hands. Turn them over. Nothing can stop you from existing. Not even you.

"George, I'm worried that you have painted such a grand picture of your "Emerald City" that those people who are thinking about suicide would rather be there than stay here amidst their confusion."

"You need not worry about that.

Religions will try to guilt you into staying there on Earth and living out your life. Such is not my intent.

I want to tell you that life and death are natural stops along your journey through personal evolution. Death is a natural part of life.

There is no shame in contemplating your death, in thinking it over, in being in awe of the wonder of death.

Your society will try to convince you that talk and thoughts of death are immoral.

I will tell you that even serious consideration of ending one's own life is shameless. It takes great courage of spirit to look at one's own mortality. It is something not many people are able to do.

It builds tremendous character to decide to die, and then decide after all to live. That process can be life altering.

Do not look down on any person you meet in life that tells you they have thought about suicide. Or attempted it. Look at them in wonder. They have dared to look past the barrier that divides our realms of existence.

Now, if you would, I would like to direct my intentions toward the friends and families and loved ones of the souls who have already ended their lives before their time.

I know the depth of your grief because just as I am bound to those on Earth who are contemplating suicide, I am as well bound to the emotions of my family and friends who I left behind when I crossed over.

I have been both required and allowed to feel their pain, to know their thoughts, and watch them grieve.

Your position is most grievous, and I greatly desire to lessen your sorrow with my words. I can tell you that your friend, your loved one, your lost one, is not in any place that you have imagined them to be, unless it is that you have imagined that they have at last come home.

The place where they now reside is one of unparalleled opportunity, hosted by spirits who are attending their deepest needs. I intend to bring you tremendous hope in telling you that you need not worry over the fate of the soul in question. You need no longer wonder.

The error of their judgment that led to their early death will not be held against them. For in this place where we spirits reside, all are welcome to the peace that is their birth-right, that goes back even to the moment of their creation.

Are you carrying the weight of guilt? Drop it. It is dead weight.

Are you experiencing loss? I wish to fill that void by telling you that no soul is ever lost.

Are you to believe that suicide victims are doomed to everlasting torment? I have seen no evidence of such. I have seen only nurturing, in degrees that you could not fathom.

Are you feeling to blame for someone's pre-mature death? There need not be any blame, or shame – only forgiveness.

Do you wonder, was there something you might have done to stop their death from occurring? Something you could have said? Listen to me, if you would shorten your grief. Do not go to the graveyard to visit your loved one. They are not there. Their spirit now walks the well lit hallways of our emerald city, comforted and comforting, learning and teaching, receiving and giving great stores of healing.

Look to the heavens to speak to them now, not to the grave. Do not lower your eyes when you speak of them, but raise your eyes and smile. Do not speak of them in hushed tones, but raise your voices in celebration of their lives!"

"George, are there any souls of those who have committed suicide that are not placed in the ward? Souls that go on to other places in the spirit realm upon crossing over?"

"Few there are, but yes."

"Tell me about their circumstances."

"It might surprise you to learn that there are certain situations in life when death is almost always preferable to life. When death has already occurred, although the body continues to walk around, so to speak."

"I don't understand what you mean by that."

"Can you think of no circumstance in life when you would prefer to die than to continue living?

Have you ever been physically tortured?

Have you been so wracked with pain that your strength of mind cannot tolerate another moment of it?

Have you known what it is like to be ill within your own mind?

Do you know the loneliness of being old and long forgotten by friends and family?

Have you known homelessness, starvation, disease?

There are souls of people who have been in these situations in life, and made the choice to end their lives, who are not placed in the ward for healing as they are not in need of that type of comfort.

They have chosen to move onward in their journey, deciding that whatever life was trying to teach them at the time was too obscure for them to pick up on. Too difficult for them to find learning amidst. Yet they understood what life was trying to do. There was no confusion about where the dividing line was between life and lesson."

"Then you are saying that it is okay to end your life in certain circumstances."

"Karen, although you keep trying to force me to take a position in the right-ness or wrong-ness of ending life, I can only repeat to you that your own society is the entity that has made it wrong. As individuals, you allow yourselves to listen to what society dictates to you. Can't you make up your own minds about it? What do you say inside of yourselves? Does it have to be right or wrong? Can a thing just be itself, in and of its own self, without a judgment call?

I did not come back through space and time to take sides in the suicide debate. I came to bring hope and understanding to a world that needs it desperately. To people who need it desperately. I came to reveal the mystery of suicide, which is this:

Whatever your choice – live or die – you will continue to live.

Whatever their choice – live or die – they will live on."

"George, there is one last thing that I want to ask you about, and that is assisted suicide. Can you shed some light on that topic for me?"

"I can indeed. Some of the most selfless people walking around on Earth have assisted in suicide. I know that you cannot accept that or even understand it, and that's okay. You needn't.

As I said already, there are certain circumstances that can occur in life when death is preferable to life. There are indeed angels amongst you that know this to be true. And upon looking into the eyes of suffering souls, they long to assist them in escaping their torment. This is a truly selfless act, in light of your laws and common ideals.

I should remind you not to be too harsh in judgment of others, as you are all walking through life in a fog and trying to get back home. Love one another, accept each other's short-comings. Give understanding above all else, whether or not you really do understand what another person is trying to do. Give understanding to each other along life's road.

"George, I have just a few more questions that I want to ask you before you go."

"Before I go where?"

"Well, before you…go away, I guess."

"Karen, I am with you always, now. I will not go away when we finish this book. Let me explain something to you that you may not understand right now. In life, I was your "Uncle George". I was not much of an uncle to you. You had a child's love to offer me and I didn't know how to go about accepting that from you. You were not alone in that regard. It was a fault of mine.

We share something now that transcends time. I am no longer your uncle. I am no longer guessing how to relate to you. One thing I have learned here is how to give and accept love, which was something that I struggled with on Earth.

I am not going away. I am part of your life now."

"Okay, then I have a few more questions before we end this book. How is that?"

"Ask away."

"Do you want to tell us more about the events that led to your early death? Are there any other details about that which we may benefit from? Can you tell me specifically why you ended your life early?"

"I came to the point in my life, the turning point you might call it, where I had become, at least in my own thoughts, a shadow of my former self. What I thought of as a counterfeit of my former self. Those thoughts came from wrong thinking, as I said earlier. I had confused my own problems with the process of life itself.

I saw my life as spiraling downward toward an inevitable death, which at that time seemed as if it was coming at me at a great speed. And I thought, if death is so inevitable, why not speed up the process? It was my attempt to take a situation that was totally out of my control, and gain what control I could. It was the only way I knew to do that – to regain control over a life where that was taken from me completely.

On the surface that rationality may seem sane, but down under the surface where truth lies, that type of thinking is shallow. Of course, I can see many things anew from this perspective. I can see choices that I might have made had I not been narrow-sighted.

I do understand that anyone thinking about taking their own life has already engaged themselves in great deals of thought and conversations. They have already given rationale to those thoughts. I am not so naïve as to think they will pick up this book and say "Good grief! What was I thinking?"

No, I am not that naïve in my world here. My purpose is to reveal the mystery – as I said already – the mystery of life, of death, and of suicide. To open minds, open them just enough to get them talking about these topics amongst yourselves.

My hope in aborting suicide is in people as a whole, as a society even, gaining new thought systems, adopting newer methods in assisting people who are feeling trapped in life. My great hope lies with your people's ability to see that what you have in place now is not working. In fact, it is so not working that you might call it an obsolete system that you have in place. Yet even being obsolete, you are still trying to beat it back to life.

Your thoughts, your ideas, your beliefs about suicide are wrong. How can you ever hope to help someone – who you already believe is doomed merely by entertaining thoughts about ending their lives – by God! How can you hope to help them when you have made them sinners by their actions?

You tip-toe around them as if they would break if they heard what you were really thinking inside.

You appease them with half truths for fear that they may commit the act and leave you feeling guilty about something you said.

You set up phone lines for them to call, with well meaning do-gooders attending the lines who try to tell them that they really don't want to kill themselves, knowing all along that they really do!

Why not try something new? Something you have not thought of before? Why not try telling them that you know they really want to end their lives? That their feelings are well founded. Try telling them how many times you, yourself, have entertained those same thoughts. Tell them that talking about death can be scary, but that you'll give it a try. That you're not sure where their soul will go if they kill themselves, and that's one of the reasons it's hard to talk about. That you're scared of them leaving you behind on Earth to live on after they're gone. Death is the great unknown, you know. Tell them that you fear it. Why not think outside the box for a change.

I can't guarantee that your trying something new will prevent all cases of suicide. But I can tell you that whatever your society is doing right now is filling up our ward with no slowing down in sight. I can guarantee you that anything would be better than the prevention methods you have in place on Earth at this time. They are simply not working. Your system needs an overhaul."

"Thank you George. Thank you for that information. I hope that you are able to find that person you said you are looking for who will assist you in the implementing of a new system down here on Earth. I am starting to believe that you really know what you're talking about."

"When the time comes, and I find the person who will assist me in that work, you will begin to see great changes taking place in regards to people wanting to end their lives early. Legislature will pass that will keep them from being treated like criminals. There will arise on your planet a newer understanding of the term "suicide". A gentler understanding.

Reader, if you feel that you are the one I have sought after to break new ground in this field, think of me and I will fill your thoughts with my insights. I will inspire to you new ideas and bring to you newer forms of energy with which to work. I am confident that with your help, together we can change the way people look at suicide forever. "

Welcome to the Emerald City

Chapter 2 in the Life After Suicide Trilogy

Welcome to the Emerald City. Welcome, welcome, one and all. You are here by special invitation, to the viewing of this magnificent place that not many eyes on Earth have looked upon.

In life, my name was George. I ended my life out of turn – an act that is referred to on Earth as suicide. After spending 25 years here in the "ward," I have decided to bring my newly gained knowledge back to people on the Earth who may benefit from some of the things I have learned here. This ward is where souls find themselves, after crossing over from life on Earth to the spirit realm. Yet the term ward hardly does it justice. It is in fact, an Emerald City.

In life, as well, I was called Uncle George by Karen, although we barely knew each other or could guess how time would bring us together after my death to write this book. She has been patient with me during these writings, open to ideas that went against everything she believed, and certainly, open to criticism as well.

The writing of the first chapter *Not Yet-The Abortion of Suicide,* brought about much controversy, and questions as well, from readers, friends, relatives, who wanted to know more about the Emerald City, as I touched on it in the first chapter, but did not go into much depth. This chapter was written in answer to those questions, and as a special favor to Karen, who seems to have been fascinated with the City since the first time I spoke about it to her.

Here then, is the second chapter of what will be 3 (Yes, 3, Karen) in this series of life occurring after suicide.

There is a gateway between our worlds, and it is called death. Further, there is a gateway leading directly to the Emerald City, which is called suicide.

You have asked me time and again, Karen, if I would show the City to you, and I have answered "no" on every account. There is no gate leading to it other than that of suicide. You cannot see it with your own eyes. I cannot take you there.

But if you will listen, I will tell you all that I know, all that I have learned of the Emerald City since first I came here.

"George, I have to ask you this question, because it is the belief of a lot of people that the act of suicide condemns the soul to damnation. Is the Emerald City hell? Or is it a place of purgation?"

The Emerald City is not either of those Karen. That is not to say that a hell or a purging does not occur for a soul, yet if it did, it would be the product only of what that soul expected to find when crossing over.

No! The Emerald City is heaven! It is rest and regeneration for the soul that has ended life out of turn, and healing, in incomparable measures.

Understand that there is a transition period that occurs just after the death and just prior to the acceptance of the healing being offered here. This transitional period is an important time – a time when the soul is discovering the weight of the mistake he has just made, feeling the consequences, understanding the error and the loss, looking back on life, and ahead to what might have been.

This transitional period is brief, even by your terms in Earth, very brief. This could be called hell, for it is terribly difficult on the soul, but even so, it is not a hell with fire and burning, eternal death or anything we have conjured up in our imaginings.

It is a trial for the soul, a learning, and yes, it is extremely intense for the soul of the suicide victim. But then, before they even know what is occurring, these wonderful spirits of love and healing are surrounding that soul, tending to, speaking to, singing to, attending to the soul, bringing understanding in many forms, showing compassion for all things done, forgiving, always forgiving, above all.

The soul is wrapped in a cloud of unspeakable nurturing, and placed in one single room at the Emerald City. The walls pulsate with crystalline rays of deep green light, and pale green light, and even while they are looking about their room where they have just been placed, astonished at the new decor where they now reside, children come to them bringing waves of laughter. Pounded by those waves, as the shoreline is pounded relentlessly by the waves of the ocean, they begin to soften, slowly soften – the better for the potter to begin His work.

"Who is the potter, George?"

The creator, of course, the creator of all things and of all times, and of all that exists. This beautiful Emerald palace glows by His design, heals by His very design, for it is not His wish that even one of His children are left unaided, even if their choice was to throw aside their gift of life, it is His wish that they go on to enjoy life in other forms, as we all do.

This beautiful green city could only have been constructed by the gentle hand of our creator, who personifies forgiveness and healing. This edifice is merely an extension of those attributes. And so, now properly softened by the laughter of the children, and their love, the soul that finds himself in a room of the Emerald City begins to heal.

"Why does the city glow green?"

The human spirit has full capabilities to heal itself and others. From the center of the chest region is an area where energies may be gathered by giving off strong feelings of love. When a human being gathers up this feeling of love and shoots it forth, he is unknowingly, unwittingly, healing.

When a human being does this consciously, on purpose, gathering up stores of compassion for others and setting them forth, a greater form of healing occurs. Greater than when it occurs unknowingly.

This energy glows green, and can be seen as such by persons who can see the human aura. This city glows green because of the enormous amounts of healing energy being exchanged here.

Here in our realm we can not only see the aura, but many other forms of energy not commonly seen while alive on the Earth.

"So, it is the healing energies being exchanged that causes the City to glow green."

Yes, to glow and pulsing in degrees of green light. That same force of healing power exists in you, by the way.

During our very first encounter after my death, I gave you a pendant to wear. It was my first attempt at showing you that the force of healing lies within you, just as it does within all people.

Karen, your people have the collective ability to build a healing facility such as ours, with nothing more than a desire to heal each other's hurts and injuries. It is within your collective realm of power to experience this magnitude of compassion on Earth as well.

"But I don't see that happening George. I don't see us making that type of progress."

You have not, up until now. However, it is well within your grasp.

"Tell me how. How is it possible for us to do that?"

I'm going to tell you 3 words, that when spoken can transform your lives. Three words that can begin your journey, lead you to that place where the healing of one another can begin.

"Feel their need." Feel their need. Look upon one another in the process of life, and feel their need.

When you meet someone in the store, when you pass another car on the road, when someone speaks to you, feel their need. The people around you, during your day, they are needing something from you, although you and they are not aware of that on a level of direct consciousness. You may be aware of it on some lower level. They are needing to be heard, to be felt, to be cared about. On the highway, they are needing to get there faster than you. They cut you off, and you mumble some inaudible something at them. Just for a moment, feel their need and let them go. It takes nothing away from you to give them that for just a moment.

In your conversations with others, they are needing to talk louder than you, faster than you, even more than you. Feel their need and let them do so. Keep silent in your thoughts while they fill their need from you. Let them drink deep.

Allow all others along your path in life to fill their void from the wellspring of your compassion. It will heal them. Gather up the compassion within that area of your chest, and allow it to flow forth. By giving that compassion and feeling their need, you will heal all those around you.

If you were each to treat one another in this way, your own walls would also glow green in your homes and in your cities.

"Do you mean that we should forget our own needs and attend to the needs of other people? What of our own needs?"

Human beings – with very few exceptions – go through their lives deciding as they go what is important to them, and what is petty. It is a rare individual who sits down and makes that distinction within their own minds early on in life – or even later on in life. A rare person who says to their own self "I will place a divider in my mind that will guide my thinking, as to what is important, and what is petty," and then goes forth from that point to live their lives according to what they have decided.

Most people make the distinction along the way, as they live. This can make insignificances in life appear as huge obstacles. Let's face it, in the scheme of life, a motor vehicle cutting you off is a pretty tiny happening. It takes up a few seconds worth of your day. However, at the time of its occurrence, you can get pretty wrapped up in the event. Yelling at the other guy, sharing gestures with them that may not show your best side.

Now, when you stop to think about that particular event – the vehicle's cutting off your path – it is a really small thing. You could decide that from now on you will feel the need of the other motorist, give him the right of way when this happens. It will not change your world one iota, besides lowering your blood pressure. You won't arrive to your destination one second earlier either way. But, your decision to feel their need sends them a different type of energy than before. It is healing energy in its most basic form. All healing power and energy begins in the heart, is bound up with human compassion, and intent, and escalates in magnitude from there.

A wise individual will read these words and begin housekeeping within their own minds, cleaning out thoughts and ideas that are out-dated by their own standards but are still being put into practice in their daily lives.

It will make a tremendous difference to those around you in your life if you will begin thinking in this new way.

Of course, your needs are important also. You have needs just like everyone else does. To progress, you must learn when your needs outweigh your own desire to heal another human being. You must decide if your own needs will ever outweigh your own desire to heal another human being, or if they will always outweigh that desire.

In general, people do not stop to think in this way. They sometimes allow another person's needs to come first, and sometimes demand their own needs take precedence. It is not common knowledge that allowing the other's need is a form of healing. I will tell you this – it is the most basic form, and all healing stems from it. All healing, on planet Earth, begins in the heart area – the heart chakra. It is a conscious intention to direct your own compassion outward and toward other people and other matter and other circumstances. It is a gathering up from within of this compassion and love (which I have told you earlier, are twin sisters) and purposefully shooting forth your own intention to heal them.

"My spirit guide Rayij told me a while back that the human imagination is more than what we guess. It seems like this is one of those times when this applies."

It is not yet time to talk about the imagination, although we will. We will cover it most thoroughly since what I have to say about it will be ground breaking in your thinking.

"One other thing, George. People who can heal on our planet sometimes refuse to take any credit for the healing, and say that only God can heal. That the healing is from God, or through Jesus from God. Can you shed some light on that for me?"

Healing is a gift from God. He designed this wonderful planet of ours so that it contained everything within it that would be needed in order for people to heal one another. The planet is very much alive. So alive, that if you had a clue to its mystery, its proper usage, even the implications of what it holds for its people, you would not be able to allow the pollution and destruction of it to continue for another moment. You would spend your every waking moment trying to stop what is now being done to it.

Planet Earth does not stop at its surface. The planet itself extends into its atmosphere, and it is directly linked to the solar system, the galaxy, and the universe, which is all very much alive, I can tell you. The planet is only a portion of its larger body.

The planet Earth is a cytoplasm. A living, radiating ball of energy. You, as an individual, may draw from that energy and allow others to draw it again from you. They may draw from the Earth as well. The Earth is a healing mechanism, and your body, mind, and spirit are fully able to convert its energy to a tangible form in order to utilize it.

Our creator has so much more in mind for us than we have dared to imagine. This body of the universe, of which the Earth is a cytoplasm, is far more intricate than the mind can grasp at. Yet know this – we are able to draw from the vast, vast resources to meet our needs, our wants, our desires, our intentions, our very imaginations (as you just mentioned).

"That is just breath-taking."

Wait, I'm not finished answering your question. You asked why people deny the healing from their own hands.

They do so – deny any part that they, themselves, play in the healing – because they are aware on some level that God is responsible for the healing energy. They do so – deny – because they are not aware of the subtle and the significant roles that they are playing. Calling out to God to heal is indeed the same thing as turning the key to the mechanism that is planet Earth. Calling out to God is like saying "Please God, allow your design that is in place already to function properly." It will function, you only need draw from the source.

Giving credit to God for healing, is like saying "Thank you God for your great design, which is the universe, of which our planet is a cell, that heals all, and we may draw from."

You see, when you know how things work, they are not so mysterious. Yet they are no less marvelous just because you now understand the basic outline of our healing universe and the role the Earth plays, and even the role that you play in healing all of nature.

The mysterious role that God plays in that of healing is also clear now. All healing comes from His great gift to us that he implemented before mankind was even created. Yet he had us in mind during His earliest musings, His earliest creations.

If you keep this outline in mind, you may unlock the secrets that you all seek. Healing is as natural as breathing air. And as natural as breathing is to the human body, healing can become a natural part of the process of your life as well.

"That is the most magnificent thing I have ever heard in my life! Even while I'm writing it down, I can't believe that it's true! But it makes perfect sense. When you said that the Earth was a cytoplasm, I was afraid that the conversation was taking a screwy turn and that I misunderstood what you were saying. Now, it turned out to be the most beautiful part of the book so far. I can't thank you enough for telling me these things.

Now let me ask you, for example, what are we to do, if we want to heal someone? What steps do we take? How do we go about it?"

The first step is in knowing that what you ask is perfectly plausible. That healing is a natural part of life and that there is a mechanism in place that allows for the healing of people, animals, plants, ecosystems, atmospheres, worlds...The first step is in having perfect faith that this is so. Faith in our creator. Your faith is the tool that will allow you to draw from the universe, and from the Earth.

"It seems like we may be getting way off base. Isn't this book supposed to be about suicide?"

No, the title of this chapter is *Welcome to The Emerald City*. It will also be about suicide, as was Chapter 1, but we will be branching off and talking about the healing nature of this city that is here in the spirit world, and the healing nature of your realm as well. You asked me questions that pertained to the elements of energy. I'm only trying to answer your questions to the best of your ability to comprehend them.

Do not be dismayed when I tell you that you have all the answers. That you do not need to communicate with me, or with your father, or your spirit guide, or relatives, asking them questions, seeking out secrets to the universe. They are already inside of you, you just have not delved down deeply enough to locate them.

While you are enjoying our communication, and it is fine that you enjoy it, continue on with it and progress from it. Keep in mind that you have all the answers.

Some of these answers are not available to you on a conscious level. You catch glimpses of them in your dreams, in your daydreams, in your fleeting thoughts, although you cannot get a grip on them with your waking mind. It is how you know that what I've just told you is true. You have always known it. It was just never put down in words for you to read and analyze before.

Now, you will never be able to deny what I have just told you. And while people everywhere may not agree that what I've said is fact, it gives the human spirit pause, because the truth of how the universe heals is embedded in our very cells. It is part of our make-up.

"Okay, so while I get that the system is already in place, how do we do it? How do we heal? How do we draw from the source?"

You begin small. To most people, it is a tremendous leap from their every day thinking to a realization that our planet and its people are part of a working machine- one that allows complete restoration of health and full faculties for every human being.

You begin slowly to allow that understanding to unfold within your mind. You feel the need of others. You gather up your compassion, and you give it to those you meet along life's way. You give it on purpose. Knowingly.

And all the while that the understanding of this mechanism is opening up to you, you gain momentum. You gain faith in your planet and in the universe and your creator. Perfect faith.

"You see, that's the problem, right there. What if I don't have perfect faith? What if I think that it may be possible to heal others, but I'm not sure? What if my faith is lacking?"

Well, Karen, if you have no faith in the process, your results are going to be inconclusive. Tell me, why is it you say that you don't feel you have the faith needed to enact the propulsion of healing? What makes your faith imperfect?

"I guess the fact that I'm imperfect."

No, no. Your imperfections have nothing to do with your belief or lack of belief in the system. Your being imperfect will not change whether or not you believe in the powers that be.

Now listen to me, listen carefully. Here is where the faith healers have it all wrong. It does not require faith in the abilities of God to perform a miracle, or receive a healing. A person can live out their whole life and not get to that level of faith. Churches will have you believe that if you do not believe in the power of God strongly enough, you will never be healed. That if you do not come to God in the right way, at the right time, or in a humble enough manner, you may or may not get your miracle.

I'm going to tell you something that is going to be new to your way of thinking. Your God, is not a man who sits up in the clouds and grants your desires if you have enough faith, and refuses them if you're not at that level of belief yet. Your God is not a man who says, "Yes, but not at this time."

Your God is a force of nature – almighty, yes – existing in a manner and form that there is no way your human mind can comprehend. A force big enough to include every thought about it that man has entertained since first man walked on the Earth. Your God is a force of nature. The most complete and expansive force that exists.

That force does not require that you believe in it. In Him. He requires nothing! He is everything.

Your God says, "Yes," at all times, in all ways. He says Yes, even before you form the question in your mind. Before you think to ask of Him. Before you are aware of your need. He says yes.

So then, you may ask why some people are healed and others are not, if He says yes to all people at all times. That is really the heart of your question I think. I can assure you that it is not on account of a lack of faith on their part.

Now, we come to that part of our earlier conversation where you asked about the human imagination, and how it all ties together with healing.

Imagination is the key to healing – the key, really, to all of life. Your imagination – which is a child's play thing.

When was the last time you allowed your imagination to run wild? To be expressed freely, without examining it? When did you last close your eyes at night and let your imagination take you on an adventure?

For many people, the answer to that question will reveal a lot about themselves. It may have been years, even decades since you have allowed that. (Not you, Karen. Your imagination runs wild during your waking hours.)

"But what is the imagination?"

The imagination is a form of energy that has never properly been described with words in the English language. I will attempt to do so now.

It is the key element in creation, in healing, and in miracle performing. It is a form of envisioning, but must be tied up with intent to utilize. Your intention and imagination, together, are extremely powerful. I will call them "intengination". What I am about to tell you about intengination has never been spoken of or written about before. It is entirely new.

Your imaginings are void of any real power, unless and until you add your intention into the equation. Once blended together, nothing is impossible.

You want to heal. You want to know how to heal. Combine your intention with your imagination, your envisioning skills with your desires, and you will unleash one of the most powerful forces of nature. If your intention is to heal, and your imagination is directed toward your intent, you can not fail.

"Can you tell me more about what the imagination really is? In terms that I can really wrap my brain around?"

Okay, what you have been brought up to believe it is, and what it actually is, are two different things. A child knows what the imagination is, even though he will not know that it is called so. He knows that the imaginary world and the real world sometimes coincide. His parents tell him over and over that they do not. They try to wring it from him, until all traces of it are behind him. They tell him it's part of growing up, to forget those imaginary thoughts, those imaginary friends. They make sure he stops talking to himself, although they usually do the same thing when alone.

A child, given full authority to exercise his imagination, will not only talk out loud, he will boisterously play out loud with invisible friends around him and toys and tools that can not be seen with the eyes. He will invent story lines and adventures.

A child, asked to pray for a sick family member or friend will stop what he is doing right then and there and begin praying out loud. He has no doubt in his mind that his prayer will be answered, that there is something mysterious in place that will answer his prayer and heal that person. He calls that something God because he has been taught to do so.

A child is in touch with his imagination only until the outside world makes him let go of it. Only until society forces him to lose his grip on it.

As an adult, then, our imagination has been out of our lives for so many years that it is difficult to find it again. Let me assure you, it can again be found.

The imagination is a tool, as is your ability to think, to feel, to reason, you are able to imagine.

Who do you "imagine" yourself to be?

What do you "imagine" lies in your future?

What state of health do you "imagine" yourself to be in?

You probably do not consciously use your ability to imagine very often; however, I can tell you that if you spent a greater portion of your time doing so, it would change your life.

Imagining is like visualizing or picturing, yet it is missing the key element, as I mentioned earlier – intent. Your intengination is one of the most powerful personal forces that you possess. It is by no accident that people become sick by the power of their own thoughts and feelings. It may take years for subconscious beliefs to manifest themselves into diseases, but they certainly will do so.

Your intengination can and will release your physical body from whatever ails it. Your intengination can and will heal others around you when you learn how to properly use it.

"Can you tell me more about how we do it, instead of just stating the fact that we can do it?"

Of course. I'm setting up the ground work for that, but first you must be able to follow along.

You now know that our planet Earth is the mechanism that enables us to heal. That it is tied to the universe, directly, and that it is all a gift from our Creator to us, which we have always known intrinsically, but probably never thought about in those terms.

To draw healing power out of the planet, we must have faith in our creator's design. To exercise this faith, we use our imagination to visualize this drawing of the healing energy up and out of the Earth, and into our own body by means of the root chakra located at the base of the spine.

"Oh my gosh! Don't tell me you're a practicing spiritualist! Just hearing you speak about the chakras is going to overturn everything I thought I knew about you."

Now just listen if you want to learn something Karen. Feel and see the healing energy entering into your body, filling every cell, every space, and filling you to capacity.

Your body may draw from the Earth at will, daily, weekly, over and over. You can condition yourself to draw energy from the Earth without even consciously thinking about it. There is an unlimited store available to you.

Your intention as to what you will do with the energy that you draw, coupled with your imagination, is what will give force, propulsion, to your motion. What you intend to do will determine all outcomes.

If you intend to heal another person, you must learn to turn on and outward your light of intent, or your globe. The globe is located at the center of your forehead. Learning to turn on the globe will animate your intention.

It will take 3 living lights to heal properly, but the globe is by far the most difficult of the 3 to learn how to use. We will discuss it last.

Once you have drawn energy from the planet, and it has filled your every space, you can shoot this energy outward from your body in several ways.

Place your right middle finger to your chest region and imagine a soft pink light shooting forth. Feel your love of all creation, of all people, and of all things. Gather that love up within yourself and allow it to shoot outward toward all of life.

Again, with your right middle finger still in place, imagine soft green light shooting outward from you, shining out and onto everyone and everything. Feel compassion within you for all people, and for all of life. Gather up what compassion you may from within you, and allow it to others.

Let the pink light, which is love, and the green light, which is human compassion, shine outward, together, but not intermingling, as they are separate.

It is your imagination that sets them forth.

Now, add your intent to your imagination, and place your left middle finger on the center of your forehead releasing pure white healing light from that area, allowing it to shine outward. Pour your bright white light on all who come in contact with you, and think very carefully about what it is you intend to do.

Your intengination will grow quickly if you exercise this ability. It is available to any person wanting to learn how to use it.

"Okay, I have another question for you George. I've been thinking about this for several days now. You said that to heal others, we can feel their need. That all healing stems from this feeling of the other person's need.

What of malicious people living here, people that intend no good to anyone else or just plain evil people? Are we expected to feel their need? To place their needs before our own?

If another Hitler incarnated here on the Earth, are you telling me that we would be expected to feel his need?"

You used the word "expected" twice in that question. Let me try to answer that as best as I can for you. You are not expected to do anything else besides what you are already doing now. You are not even expected to do that. Nothing is expected of you. Who would expect it?

Are you thinking that God watches your every action and holds expectation over them?

You are on the Earth by your own design my friend. You have come again to live life in the physical because of your own expectations. You have chosen life in a physical human body, over all the other forms and means of life that you could have drawn from because of the specific modes of learning available to your soul, guaranteed you by the unique relationships that exist on the planet Earth.

In short, you have come here for the learning experience. Because of the other people inhabiting the planet, you are explicitly guaranteed that you will undergo encounters with those other people. What you do, what you say, and what you decide that you will feel in the moment, while you are relating to those other people, will determine the learning experience.

You do not have to do anything that you don't want to. That is a basic rule of life, although not many people look at it that way. There are no requirements, besides live and die. Or live, and then live again.

Now, you told me that you wanted to learn how to heal. That you wanted to understand the basic mechanics of healing and you asked for details. Not just that we can do it, but how.

Okay, that's a noble undertaking.

I did not say for you to bow down to the other's need. I said to feel their need. To acknowledge the need. To stop what you're doing in the process of your day, and look at their need. Consciously saying, yes, I see that there is a fundamental need therein.

Then, I said that the choice was yours to make, whether you would place your own needs above the other person, to decide if your own need would outweigh your desire to heal.

Life is certainly full of malicious people, even evil-intending people who you have a good chance of encountering during your life. Remember, that you asked me how to heal. Remember that while I'm telling you these things.

Will you bow to the other's need, when their intent is not a good one? Certainly, no greater love has a man than to lay down his life for another. No greater power can be transferred from one soul to another, than the power of love, which can heal.

"You are losing me in this conversation."

Okay, then let's get back to the question Karen. You asked what will be expected of you when you meet another person in life who is not a good person. I told you that there is nothing required of you, ever. But remember, you told me that you want to heal. Nothing is required of you in life, but to show up – unless you have expectations of your own.

"You're telling me that I should feel their need no matter who they are or what their intention, even if they mean me harm or want to kill me."

If you wish to heal.

"If someone puts a gun to my head."

Who could be more desperate for healing?

"I'm beginning to understand. Just beginning to."

That's good then because it will grow inside of you from there. Now, if we have finished with our talk about healing and have planted some seeds for your planet's understanding, we should move on to our final chapter in this trilogy of life after suicide. Do you have any last questions about healing?

"I can't think of any other questions. You have satisfied my curiosity fully, although I'm not sure yet that I can do the things that you say, I'm certain that it's possible."

Then, we should move on.

A Life That is Real

Chapter 3 in the
Life After Suicide Trilogy

George, it feels to me that we have really gotten off track in Chapter 2, and I'm wondering if this chapter will lead us back to the real topic of this book which is life after suicide."

Yes, I want to return us now to the Emerald City as we discuss the soul's journey as it is healed, and its eventual dismissal from the City's charge.

No soul can stay in the City forever, as I told you earlier in Chapter 1 that life is not stagnant. Its very definition means ever-changing.

It is important, before we re-enter the City, that we talk about forms of life and of the cosmic wheel and of what I would like to call the place that is our true home. Some call this place heaven. Let us refer to it as such – heaven.

Just as when I told you that our Creator is a force of nature big enough to include every thought about it that man has ever entertained, so is it with heaven. It is more than a place, it is a state of mind. It exists outside of the boundaries that you are presently able to construct or comprehend.

Heaven is where all of life in every form originated, and it is the place (and state of mind) where all return to in their proper time, repeatedly.

Life on Earth, human existence, is one of a billion, billion forms of life, originating in heaven, returning again, repeatedly.

Human existence is a vehicle which your soul utilizes for growth, particularly because of the close proximity of relationship, each with another. We choose to come to Earth, to live out a lifetime, because of what me might learn about ourselves, what we may experience of ourselves, and precisely what we may rediscover about ourselves over and over again.

Do not allow yourself to believe that you are who you have been in this lifetime. The greatest secret is that you are who and what you are becoming. You are who and what you dream you can be.

There are times in life when you must look back on your actions to recognize that they do not reflect who you are, that they no longer reflect who you are, even, that they never did reflect who you are.

Each of us finds our self on planet Earth because we have selected physical life above all other forms of life, for our soul's present state of growth.

Opportunities arise in life that you will misconstrue as problems. You will call them calamities, tragedies. You will seek to turn from them, to run from them. Yet, only in your turning toward them and seeking out their deeper meaning will you gain the growth you sought after all those long years ago, when you selected a physical life. And, only by remembering that you will again return to your true home – unharmed, intact – will you retain the strength of mind and body needed to call the tragedies of life true opportunities.

Life on Earth is not real. Read that. Not real.

"Please George, can you tell me how we can learn to see opportunity in the tragedies of life?"

When misfortune befalls you, remember that somewhere in the very heart of what is happening, wisdom exists. A knowledge that you would otherwise not have come by.

When you look around at others in the midst of their own misfortunes, remember that they are also seeking after wisdom and knowledge of their own kind. Their souls seek growth as well. It is the very reason we all exist together at this point in time.

Now it is time for us to return to the Emerald City with this new understanding of life fresh in your memory. Remember these things that I have told you. Remember them, as they have the ability to carry you through the calamities of your own life.

"Thank you George. Thank you. Now I want to ask you another question if I may. If life on Earth is illusion, as you say – and as I have always believed incidentally – and what we return to after this is the life that is real, why are you so concerned with suicide, and with aborting suicide? Aren't we better off returning to our true home where we can choose our next form of life?"

You're missing the point Karen! You're looking right past my whole purpose.

"Which is what?"

As I told you several times already, my purpose is to reveal the mystery of life, of death, and of suicide.

"Ah, yes, I keep forgetting. And the mystery of each, is what?"

The mystery of life is that it never ends.
The mystery of death is that it does not occur.

The mystery of suicide will be revealed by the end of this book.

We are returning now to the Emerald City. Please, no more questions while we travel with a newly arriving soul through his earliest encounters at the City.

I have described for you how the soul must suffer the trials of the transition period, then, to find that they are adjusting to the placement in their room. Healing begins immediately for that soul. Children are sent to their side.

"George, describe for me what a room would look like in the Emerald City. Are there windows? A Bed? Pictures on the wall?"

It is nothing like you would recognize.

"Then what is there in the room?"

Waves of unconditional love. Music of a kind, that were you to hear a moment's worth you would burst into tears of joy. Colors and colors that fill all space.

"Is there anything for the soul to do while in the room?"

Yes, heal.

"I mean, is there a chair to sit on, or a bed to lie on? A kitchen to cook in? What do the souls do there? What is there to occupy or to entertain them?"

They begin their healing journey. They are absorbed in mind and emotion, not with a physical body any longer. There is no television with a game system attached to occupy them Karen. They are mentally and emotionally absorbed in treatment.

Great stores of knowledge are made available to them foremost. New understandings that overturn earlier thought systems. Expanded states of mind which make physical consciousness pale in comparison.

Are you beginning to understand what there is to do? There is a great dawning of wisdom taking place within the soul. Realization, acknowledgement, acceptance – these things and so much more.

What is there to occupy them, you ask? The marvelous beginnings of a new life.

Oh yes, there will still be the lingering of the past regret, the loss, the emotional tearing asunder, but those are the remnants of the soul's physical senses which are fading quickly from their pool of necessity.

Newer senses are being developed at an incredible rate of speed. Senses that originate within the mind and the very fabric of their being.

"Like what? What kinds of newer senses?"

Many that we often think of as paranormal or senses of the psyche. Now let's try to get through this with as little interruption as possible if we may. If you have questions I will try to answer them later.

The soul, which had been living within the constraints of the physical body for so long, does not make the adjustment back to spirit instantaneously, especially after the event of ending their Earthly life early. The premature ending of their human life prolongs the adjustment. It complicates their return to spirit since there is so much attachment for them to their life on the Earth, including the emotions of family and loved ones. Do you remember that I told you that I am bound to the Earth by my action? To my family members and to those on Earth who contemplate suicide? So too, are the souls in the Emerald City – both allowed and required to feel the pain of their loved ones and the confusion of others who seek to leave life before its proper time.

Yet, their physical senses will fade and their spiritual senses will grow in intensity.

As these new senses grow, as new understandings dawn, the soul will blossom in its new form of life, for you see, life is eternal. It may and it certainly will change in form, over and again, but it cannot be extinguished. At the moment of what you refer to on Earth as "death," you will still live. There will not be even a moment of time when you will enter a darkness and come out again into the light. Not even a nano-second of time when you will undergo a dying off of your old self and a rebirth of your new self. It is the illusion of death that makes it seem so to you. The reality is, that life is a constant. Many souls even enter the realm of the spirit before they fully leave their body. These people can tell you that there is no death, indeed, many have tried to tell you that. It is the illusion, the grand illusion of death, that keeps from you a true understanding.

"George, how long does a soul typically stay in the Emerald City?"

We do not measure out time in years or by the movement of planets through the solar system.

A soul will journey through the phases of the City until healing has taken place and the soul seeks further learning, or wishes to move on in service to others. Many tenants of the City dedicate a certain amount of their work to those in the physical world who are considering ending their lives early.

Yet, sooner or later, eventually, all souls who have come to the ward by means of suicide must leave the City, and even those souls who have left the City to work with men and women on the Earth will have to move on from the charge of the ward.

Just as I told you that you can not physically visit the ward because of the highs and lows of energies being exchanged, so too, the tenants of the ward cannot linger here indefinitely. When healing has taken place, when service to others has been fulfilled, there is life, of another kind, waiting again around the corner.

There are new opportunities to learn, to serve, and to become. Always, there are new chances to become.

– Such as life is on Earth. This is your present opportunity to learn, to serve, and to become. –

"Do some souls come back to Earth again to live out another life?"

I did not say that I would reveal the mystery of reincarnation. It is enough to unveil the truth of life existing after suicide. It should be enough to uncover this great hope for mankind.

"A billion, billion forms?"

It truly boggles the mind.

"And of those billion, billion, I have chosen physical life this time."

Because of the unique opportunities the planet and its people afford.

"Then there must have been a good reason for my choice. Something important that I wanted to do. Some specific growth I felt that I needed."

You are beginning to understand.

"I decided to come down to the Earth – I chose it – and in so doing, I sought a higher wisdom in the trials and workings of life."

Exactly.

"Problems arise throughout my lifetime because I have drawn them."

So to speak.

"And I draw the problems to myself because I seek their deeper meaning. I seek the gift that they contain. The wisdom."

Be careful. Once you start talking like that others will not know what to make of you.

"But I understand it now! I get it! We are all here because we have chosen to live together – to co-exist even – for our own evolution. We are all just trying to remember what it is we're doing here, blundering our way through, trying to get back home."

To the life that is real.

"That's it then, isn't it? That's what you've come here to tell us. You're through, aren't you?"

I've said all I've needed to and everything I've promised.

"I thought it would be a longer book."

Think of it this way – I won't keep you up past midnight any more.

"I feel almost sad that it's coming to a close. I never really believed we would get to the end."

Then I won't mind telling you that this is only the first of our books that we will write together.

"It is? What do you mean? There is going to be another?"

Others.

"Oh my gosh!"

Later. They will come later. You have other work to occupy yourself with at this time.

Thank you for your long hours sitting up at night with a flashlight and pen. Thank you for the mornings you spent yawning through your breakfast. There is no way I can show you my appreciation for what you have done for me.

"Are you kidding? What you have shared with me here means more than you know. Some of the things you have told me have changed my thinking forever. Changed my life in some small manners. You never know, they might change them in greater measure as time goes by. I am the one who is grateful. I feel a certain calm now that you are with me, as you said, always now.

Thank you George. Thank you and good-bye."

Farewell my child, I will visit with you on the balcony when your time allows and when you are ready to begin our next project together.

And farewell to you, who have chosen to join us on our journey beyond the veil of dimension. I wish you God-speed on your own pilgrimage, back to the spirit world where you truly will find a life. A life that is real.

About the Author

Karen Peebles

My love for writing began early in life when I started writing poetry and short stories at age 8. That love grew into something quite passionate over the years. Father's Day cards with poems enclosed turned into magazine articles, poetry anthologies, newspaper editorials, anything I could do to get my writing into the hands of other people.

In 2006 I was approached by Publish America to have my first book published, Death is the Daybreak, which I gratefully accepted. Soon after that time, I began self-publishing my own books on the online website lulu.com. I am enjoying a moderate amount of success with the self-published titles, promoting them on various websites that advertise on the google search engine free of charge.

My self-published books range in subject material from historical photographs to organic gardening, natural healing, puzzle solving techniques, simple how-to books, and my personal favorite, life after death, which I am most passionate about.

Throughout my life I have enjoyed hundreds of visits from members of my family who have "died". Through these visits, I have come to feel that what we think of as death is really a new adventure. My family members on the other side of the veil have revealed to me what I have come to call "secrets of the universe". Wonders. These experiences have changed my life.

At this time, I am 42 years old, I am recently widowed and home school my 2 children in our home in Lebanon, Missouri. Our open schedule allows us to travel locally and enjoy many freedoms that would not be available to us otherwise.

Other Books Published
by
Ozark Mountain Publishing, Inc.

Conversations with Nostradamus, Volume I, II, III................by Dolores Cannon
Jesus and the Essenes..by Dolores Cannon
They Walked with Jesus..by Dolores Cannon
Between Death and Life... by Dolores Cannon
A Soul Remembers Hiroshima..by Dolores Cannon
Keepers of the Garden..by Dolores Cannon
The Legend of Starcrash..by Dolores Cannon
The Custodians..by Dolores Cannon
The Convoluted Universe - Book One, Two, Three..............by Dolores Cannon
I Have Lived Before...by Sture Lönnerstrand
The Forgotten Woman..by Arun & Sunanda Gandhi
Luck Doesn't Happen by Chance...................................by Claire Doyle Beland
Mankind - Child of the Stars..............................by Max H. Flindt & Otto Binder
The Gnostic Papers..by John V. Panella
Past Life Memories As A Confederate Soldier.........................by James H. Kent
Holiday in Heaven...by Aron Abrahamsen
Is Jehovah An E.T.?...by Dorothy Leon
The Ultimate Dictionary of Dream Language............................by Briceida Ryan
The Essenes - Children of the Light...............by Stuart Wilson & Joanna Prentis
Power of the Magdalene................................by Stuart Wilson & Joanna Prentis
Rebirth of the Oracle.................................by Justine Alessi & M. E. McMillan
Reincarnation: The View from Eternity......by O.T. Bonnett, M.D. & Greg Satre
The Divinity Factor..by Donald L. Hicks
What I Learned After Medical School ....by O.T. Bonnett, M.D.
Why Healing Happens..by O.T. Bonnett, M.D.
A Journey Into Being...by Christine Ramos, RN
Discover The Universe Within You...by Mary Letorney
Worlds Beyond Death..by Rev. Grant H. Pealer
Let's Get Natural With Herbs..by Debra Rayburn
The Enchanted Garden...by Jodi Felice
My Teachers Wear Fur Coats........................by Susan Mack & Natalia Krawetz
Seeing True...by Ronald Chapman
Elder Gods of Antiquity..by M. Don Schorn
Legacy of the Elder Gods...by M. Don Schorn

Continue for more books by Ozark Mountain Publishing, Inc.

For more information about any of the above titles, soon to be released titles, or other items in our catalog, write or visit our website:

OZARK MOUNTAIN PUBLISHING

PO Box 754
Huntsville, AR 72740
www.ozarkmt.com
1-800-935-0045/479-738-2348 Wholesale Inquiries Welcome